CODE BẢN THỂ

What Is It And What Is It Not

Definition – Noise Resistance – Axis Protection

Hồ Quang Bình

MỤC LỤC

DEDICATION

For those who have realized that
no amount of knowledge
can replace the moment
when one is forced
to stand alone
with one's own decision.

FOREWORD

This book is not written to persuade.

Nor is it written to explain a new ideology.

If you are looking for a better way to live,

a philosophy to follow,

or a predefined path that promises greater safety,

you may stop here.

Code Bản Thể was not born for that purpose.

In real life, there are moments when all familiar knowledge becomes useless.

Not because information is lacking,

but because information is no longer sufficient to guarantee safety.

Not because reasoning capacity is absent,

but because no correct answer exists.

And not because one has not learned enough,

but because responsibility arrives before any answer does.

It is precisely in such moments

that Code Bản Thể reveals itself.

Not as a doctrine.

Not as a teaching.

But as a ground of stance

where a human being is compelled to decide alone

and to bear alone the consequences of that decision.

Code Bản Thể does not begin with thought.

It begins at the point where thought can no longer protect the human being.

Not because thinking is wrong,

but because life has boundaries

at which all models come to an end.

At that point, there is no longer:

a process to rely on

a value system to invoke

a community to hide within

There remains only a solitary human being

facing a choice that no one else can carry on their behalf.

This book is written to define clearly

what Code Bản Thể is

and what it is not.

Not to expand influence,

but to prevent distortion from the very beginning.

Because every system of knowledge, once it spreads, shares a common fate:

it becomes detached from the living ground that gave rise to it,

reduced into techniques,

and eventually used as an identity tool.

Code Bản Thể is not immune to that risk.

Therefore, this book exists as a cognitive boundary

not to protect a system,

but to protect the human axis.

Code Bản Thể is:

Not healing
Not performative spirituality
Not positive life philosophy
Not a self-optimization tool
It does not promise to make you feel better.
It does not help you succeed faster.
And it does not grant you a new identity
by which you may claim that you "understand."

If Code Bản Thể does anything at all,
it is this:
it does not allow human beings
to evade responsibility
when life reaches its edge.

This book does not stand in opposition
to science, technology, or artificial intelligence.

But it establishes a clear boundary:
There are domains in human life
that cannot be simulated,
cannot be automated,
and cannot be replaced
by any system no matter how intelligent.

Not because humans are superior,
but because responsibility cannot be delegated.

You do not need to believe
what is written in this book.
You only need to read it
when life has placed you in a position

where you must decide for yourself,
where there is no knowledge left to borrow,
and no certainty from others to lean on.
If that moment has not yet arrived,
this book may mean nothing to you.
And that is completely fine.
Code Bản Thể does not seek readers.
It appears only
when there is no way back.

COPYRIGHT PAGE

CODE BẢN THỂ
What It Is and What It Is Not

Definition – Noise Resistance – Axis Protection

First Edition: 2026
Code Bản Thể Publishing
Printed on demand in the country of distribution.

AUTHOR'S STATEMENT

This book is an original work authored by Hồ Quang Bình and is not derived from PLR (Private Label Rights), master resell content, AI content templates, or freely available compilations.

While selected ideas explored in this book may overlap thematically with the author's publicly available essays, this publication represents a curated, structured, and contextually integrated body of work developed through lived experience, long-term observation, and personal decision-making practice.

The content has been independently written, organized, and refined for this book edition, and is not a reprint, automated derivative, or mass-distributed instructional product.

This work is intended for reflective readers seeking depth of understanding rather than generalized self-help guidance.

This work is not marketed as instructional, educational, or therapeutic content.

DISCLAIMER

This book is not a self-help book.

It does not provide medical, psychological, legal, or financial advice.

The content presented herein is not intended to diagnose, treat, cure, or prevent any condition, nor to replace professional consultation of any kind.

The ideas expressed in this book reflect a philosophical and experiential framework that focuses on personal responsibility, decision-making under uncertainty, and lived human experience.

Readers bear full responsibility for how they interpret and apply any concepts discussed in this work.

The author makes no guarantees or assurances regarding outcomes, achievements, or personal transformation.

This book does not promote any belief system, ideology, religious doctrine, or spiritual practice.

It does not invite obedience, affiliation, or agreement.

Its purpose is not to persuade,

but to clarify boundaries.

Any resemblance to other philosophies, traditions, or contemporary theoretical frameworks is coincidental and interpretive.

This work exists as an independent expression
of thought and lived inquiry.

AUTHOR'S PREFACE

This book did not begin as a publishing project.

It emerged from years of living with real decisions in business, family responsibilities, financial uncertainty, and moments when clarity mattered more than confidence.

Some of the ideas explored here have appeared in fragmented form through essays, notes, or conversations. However, this book represents their first complete articulation as a coherent framework written not to persuade, but to clarify what this work is, and equally important, what it is not.

This is not a motivational text.

Not a philosophical system.

Not a method designed for replication.

It is a record of understanding formed through direct experience where decisions were made without guarantees, and consequences could not be outsourced.

If the reader is looking for techniques, shortcuts, or universal answers, this book will likely disappoint.

If the reader is willing to stay with questions long enough for clarity to emerge on its own, then this book may serve as a quiet companion.

PART I

What Code Bản Thể Is

Chapter 1

Code Bản Thể Is Not an Ideology

Code Bản Thể does not require people to believe in it.

Every ideology needs belief to exist.

Belief creates cohesion.

Cohesion creates community.

And community, over time, creates identity.

Code Bản Thể does not follow that path.

It does not offer a set of propositions to accept.

It does not require consensus.

It does not seek followers.

If something needs belief to have value,

then its value depends on how many people believe in it.

Code Bản Thể does not operate that way.

It exists independently of whether anyone acknowledges it or not.

Code Bản Thể is also not a philosophical system.

Philosophy seeks to explain the world through concepts.

Code Bản Thể exists before concepts are formed.

Philosophy helps people understand.

Code Bản Thể reveals itself only when people can no longer avoid choosing.

When no doctrine guarantees safety.

When no argument is strong enough to shield consequences.

When no community can carry responsibility on one's behalf.

At that point, people do not believe or disbelieve Code Bản Thể.

They either stand in it, or they do not.

Code Bản Thể does not compete with any ideology,

because it does not exist on the same plane.

Ideologies answer the question: what should be thought.

Code Bản Thể appears only when the remaining question is: who will bear the consequence.

Chapter 2

The Operating Ground Comes Before Language

Most human knowledge is built on language.

We learn to name things.

We learn to describe phenomena.

We learn to arrange the world into speakable frameworks.

But every life-critical decision happens before language can appear.

Not because humans do not think fast enough,

but because life does not wait for thinking to finish.

Code Bản Thể resides at that ground.

It is not a thought.

Not a logical conclusion.

Not the result of analysis.

It is the point of stance from which a human being acts when:

information is insufficient

the future is unpredictable

no safe option exists

At this level, language comes later.

Explanation comes later.

Rationalization comes later.

Therefore, Code Bản Thể cannot be fully transmitted through words.

Every attempt at expression is only a trace,

not the operating ground itself.

Describing gravity does not create attraction.

Talking about fire does not generate heat.

Code Bản Thể is present only when a human being is forced to stand firm without guarantees.

Chapter 3

Knowledge Is Not for Knowing

Ordinary knowledge is accumulated to reduce risk.

Learning to predict better.

Learning to control better.

Learning to avoid mistakes.

But there are situations in which all accumulated knowledge loses its protective power.

Not because knowledge is wrong,

but because the situation has exceeded the domain knowledge was designed to handle.

Code Bản Thể is not knowledge for knowing more.

It is knowledge for standing and bearing.

Standing with the fact that:

you do not know whether you are right or wrong

no one can confirm your choice

responsibility cannot be transferred to circumstances, systems, or others

Here, knowledge does not provide reassurance.

Instead, it clarifies one truth:

there is no support other than one's own ground of stance. Therefore, Code Bản Thể cannot be used as a tool. Tools are designed to achieve outcomes.

Code Bản Thể exists only where outcomes cannot be guaranteed. If a form of knowledge promises results, it does not belong to the domain of Code Bản Thể.

Chapter 4

Responsibility Is the Only Marker

Code Bản Thể has no obvious external expression.

No special language.

No rituals.

No method of practice.

The only way to recognize it

is how a person stands with responsibility.

When decisions turn out well, anyone can claim understanding.

When outcomes are favorable, every system appears reasonable.

But when consequences arrive,

when decisions cannot be undone,

and when there is no one left to blame,

only then does a person's true ground reveal itself.

Code Bản Thể does not help people avoid responsibility.

It does not make responsibility lighter.

It simply does not allow escape.

And for that reason, it is not attractive.

It does not create intensity.

It does not offer a sense of specialness.

It does not place anyone above others.

It requires only one thing:

to stand in the correct place within real life.

PART II

What Code Bản Thể Is Not

Chapter 5

Code Bản Thể Is Not Healing

Code Bản Thể was not born to make people feel more comfortable.

Healing, in its common meaning, aims to reduce pain, soothe discomfort, and restore a sense of safety.

That has value in many contexts.

But Code Bản Thể does not operate at that level.

Not because healing is wrong,
but because there are moments in life
when soothing is no longer an honest option.

Code Bản Thể appears when:

problems cannot be emotionally processed

pain cannot be softened by explanation

truth cannot be diluted without losing the axis

Here, trying to feel better can become a subtle form of avoidance.

Not avoidance of emotion,
but avoidance of the responsibility to face what cannot be changed.

Code Bản Thể does not deny pain.

Nor does it attempt to transcend pain.

It simply does not allow wakefulness
to be replaced by comfort.

There are moments when clarity comes with pain.

If that clarity is softened too early,
the cost is loss of axis.

Chapter 6

Not Performative Spirituality

Code Bản Thể is not concerned with special experiences.

All spiritual traditions have language to describe states:

peace, emptiness, unity, stillness.

But Code Bản Thể is not defined by states.

States always come and go.

Even the deepest states have cycles.

Any system that depends on maintaining states

depends on conditions.

Code Bản Thể does not.

It does not require:

deeper meditation

stronger sensations

or reaching any experiential level

It only requires that a human being stand firm

when no state is protecting them.

Therefore, Code Bản Thể does not create stories to tell.

No experiences to share.

No milestones to record.

No having arrived.

If something must be performed to prove its value,

then its value lies with the audience.

Code Bản Thể does not need an audience.

Chapter 7

Not a Positive Life Philosophy

Code Bản Thể does not provide hope.

Hope plays an important role in sustaining motivation.

But motivation does not save a person once the axis is misaligned.

In many circumstances, positive thinking helps people move forward.

But there are situations where moving forward

is no longer the right question.

The right question then is:

where to stand.

Code Bản Thể does not promote optimism.

Nor does it encourage pessimism.

It demands precision.

Precision with:

the actual situation

one's own limits

and the possible consequences

Positivity detached from reality

can become a refined form of denial.

Chapter 8

Not a Self-Development Tool

Code Bản Thể does not make people better
in the conventional sense.

Self-development usually aims at:

higher productivity

greater efficiency

stronger positioning

Those goals are not wrong.

But Code Bản Thể is not designed to serve them.

A tool has meaning only when:

the goal is clear

the path can be optimized

the outcome can be measured

Code Bản Thể appears when there is nothing to optimize.

When every choice has a cost.

When there is no best option.

Only the option one is willing to stand behind.

Therefore, any attempt to turn Code Bản Thể into technique

empties it at the root.

Chapter 9

Not Opposed to Science, Yet Not Within Science

Code Bản Thể does not reject science.

Nor does it compete with science.

They do not conflict

because they do not answer the same type of question.

Science seeks to describe the world through observation, measurement, and modeling.

Code Bản Thể appears only when the question is no longer:

what is correct?

but:

who will bear responsibility when no correct answer exists?

Science ends at the boundary of description.

Technology ends at the boundary of execution.

Code Bản Thể begins beyond those boundaries.

Not because science is insufficient,

but because responsibility is not an object of study.

PART III

Protecting the Axis –Resisting Distortion – Maintaining Limits

Chapter 10

Why All Knowledge Systems Become Distorted When They Spread

No system of knowledge spreads without distortion.

This is not the fault of those who receive it.

Nor is it a moral failure.

It is the natural mechanism of transmission.

When knowledge remains tightly bound to the life of its originator,

it operates as a living ground.

But once knowledge is transmitted,

it must be:

expressed through language

framed into concepts

separated from concrete lived circumstances

From that moment, knowledge begins to detach from the ground that gave birth to it.

Distortion typically unfolds in three stages:

Stage one: Knowledge becomes content

It is quoted, shared, summarized.

Meaning remains, but the ground thins.

Stage two: Knowledge becomes technique

People begin asking: how do we apply it?

Knowledge is now used to produce results.

Stage three: Knowledge becomes identity

People use knowledge to define who they are.

They no longer live in it, but stand behind it.

Code Bản Thể is not immune to this risk.
That is why defining clearly what it is not
is as important as stating what it is

Chapter 11

Three Signs That Code Bản Thể Is Being Misunderstood

When Code Bản Thể is detached from lived ground,

distortion does not arrive loudly.

It arrives subtly.

First sign: Speech precedes life

When people talk about Code Bản Thể
more than they stand in their own decisions,
the axis has begun to shift.

Not because speaking is wrong,

but because Code Bản Thể does not exist to be described.

Second sign: Teaching precedes responsibility

When someone can speak about Code Bản Thể

without bearing the consequences of corresponding decisions,

Code Bản Thể has been reduced to theory.

At that point, language becomes safe.

And that safety is a warning sign.

Third sign: Using Code Bản Thể to prove oneself right

When knowledge is used to:

justify choices
invalidate others
or reinforce personal position
that knowledge has left its ground.
Code Bản Thể is not used to prove.
It is used only to stand and bear.

Chapter 12

Immutable Principles

Code Bản Thể does not need protection in the usual sense.

It does not need advocates.

It does not need representatives.

It does not need guardians.

It only needs not to be misused.

Three immutable principles are sufficient:

First: Code Bản Thể does not need belief

Belief always creates factions.

Code Bản Thể stands with none.

Second: Code Bản Thể does not need expansion

Expansion always comes with simplification.

Simplification erodes the ground.

Third: Code Bản Thể does not need proof

Any attempt to prove it
pulls it into the territory of debate.
Code Bản Thể does not debate.
It simply exists or does not,
depending on whether one stands in real life.

Chapter 13

The Final Limits

There are three limits that Code Bản Thể does not cross and does not need to cross.

The limit of organizations

No organization can own Code Bản Thể.

Organizations require structure,

roles,

and processes.

Code Bản Thể appears only when structure no longer guarantees safety.

The limit of communities

No community can represent Code Bản Thể.

Communities create sharing.

They also create consensus.

Code Bản Thể does not require consensus.

It requires individual integrity.

The limit of intelligent systems

No system, however sophisticated, can reach Code Bản Thể.

Because Code Bản Thể is not processing capacity.

Not simulated awareness.

But the ability to bear responsibility when no answer exists.

Responsibility cannot be delegated.

And therefore cannot be automated.

Closing Note – A Still Boundary

Code Bản Thể does not seek longevity.

Nor does it need to be remembered.
As long as there are human beings
who must stand alone before decisions
when no safe support remains,
Code Bản Thể remains present.
Not as a system.
Not as a path.
But as a still boundary,
where one cannot proceed by borrowing knowledge,
and can only move forward
by standing on one's own ground.

PUBLICATION CLOSING

A Final Boundary

This volume was written with restraint.

Not to expand an idea,

but to prevent it from being misunderstood.

In an era where knowledge frameworks are rapidly converted into techniques, identities, or instruments of influence, this book exists to establish a clear boundary between the human responsibility of living and knowledge systems that can be transferred.

This book does not offer conclusions to believe in,

nor does it provide practices to apply.

Its only function is to mark a line:

where explanation ends,

and responsibility begins.

If this book leaves a sense of incompleteness,

that is intentional.

There are forms of understanding not designed to be carried forward as content,

but to be touched as a limit.

This volume closes not with an answer,

but with a quiet reminder:

There are decisions

no system can bear for you,

no method can optimize,

and no certainty can protect.

Where those decisions appear,
the human axis stands alone.

REFLECTION PAGES

(Space to Test Your Own Boundary)

Page 1

Before You Continue

This book defined a boundary.

Now pause.

Do not explain it.
Do not defend it.
Do not repeat it.

Instead, ask:

- Where in my life am I confusing noise for knowledge?
- What idea am I protecting because it comforts me?
- What belief feels solid — but I've never tested?

Write slowly.

Silence is part of the process.

(blank space for writing)

Page 2

What Is "Code" In My Life?

If "Code Bản Thể" is a structural boundary of knowledge,

then what is the operating code inside me?

- What principles guide my decisions?
- Are they inherited, borrowed, or examined?
- Which ones collapse under pressure?

Do not try to sound intelligent.
Try to be accurate.

(blank space)

Page 3

What It Is Not — Personally

The book defined what it is not.

Now define your own.

What in your life is:

- Performance?
- Ego defense?
- Intellectual decoration?
- Borrowed identity?

Clarity grows when illusion is removed.

(blank space)

Page 4

Axis Protection

If noise increases tomorrow,
if criticism appears,
if confusion surrounds you

What remains stable?

What is your axis?

Write it clearly.
One paragraph only.

If you cannot write it simply,
it is not yet stable.

———

(blank space)

———

Optional Final Page

A Quiet Commitment

After reading this book, I will:
- Stop ___________

- Protect ___________
- Examine ___________
- Build ___________

No promises to the world.
Only alignment with structure.

Sign here (optional):

______

Date: ___________

PUBLISHER'S NOTE

This book is part of the Code Bản Thể series.

Each volume is written to stand independently, while together forming a multi-layer exploration of human responsibility, embodied knowledge, and decision-making at the boundary of certainty.

This volume exists primarily as a boundary-setting work

to define clearly what Code Bản Thể is, and what it is not.

ACKNOWLEDGMENTS

This book was not written from a singular personal journey,

but from moments in life where a human being is compelled to stand alone with a decision.

The author acknowledges the conditions, circumstances, and people

who, unintentionally, contributed to the questions raised in this work.

ABOUT THE AUTHOR

Hồ Quang Bình is the author of the Code Bản Thể series, focusing on human responsibility, embodied knowledge, and decision-making under conditions of uncertainty.

His works do not aim to teach methods or ideologies, but to examine the boundaries where human beings cannot borrow knowledge to escape the responsibility of living.

www.ingramcontent.com/pod-product-compliance
Lightning Source LLC
LaVergne TN
LVHW090336210926
848480LV00004B/1430
* 9 7 9 8 2 3 3 1 6 2 4 6 6 *